In Killdeer's Field

In Killdeer's Field

Steven R. Cope

Wind Publications
2002

In Killdeer's Field. Copyright © 2002 Steven R. Cope. All rights reserved. Printed in the United States of America. No part of this book may be reproduced without permission except in the case of brief quotations embodied in critical articles and reviews. For information address Wind Publications, 600 Overbrook Drive, Nicholasville, KY 40356 or e-mail info@windpub.org.

First Edition

ISBN 1-893239-04-7

Library of Congress Control Number 2001094480

Acknowledgments

The author thanks the editors of the books and magazines where many of these poems first appeared, some in slightly different form:

Albatross— "Pastoral"
Aura— "Landover Beach"
Buffalo Spree— "The Dig" and "Fete At Twilight"
Cincinnati Poetry Review— "Nightwalker"
Cold Mountain Review— "Ohshon"
Confrontation— "Death Of W."
Cumberland Poetry Review— "A Burial"
Cumberlands— "Tyros"
Epiphany— "Museum"
Eureka Literary Magazine— "Appalache," "Fishing For Home," and "Gaming"
The Hollins Critic— "Hunting With Professors" and "The Meaning Of The Moon"
International Poetry Review— "Aesop Come To Perch," "The Fall Of '86," and "Bells On The Mountain"
The Journal of Kentucky Studies— "Old Crow"
Kansas Quarterly— "Of Whitman, Reclining"
Kentucky Poetry Review— "The Ritual" and "The Art Of Seeing"
The Literary Review— "Freud" and "Once In A Blue Moon"
Lost Creek Letters— "Bar Verse"
The MacGuffin— "The Hunters"
Pine Mountain Sand & Gravel— "Communal"
Poem— "The Country In Which All Others Are But States Of Mind" and "Man-Song"

Poetry Northwest— "What We Have Heard On High" and "The Birds In My Window"
Scripsit— "The Other Word," "Sleeping Out," "Taking My Country With Me," and "Tornadium"
Stone Country— "Flight" and "Sacred Cows"
Sun Dog— "Indian Summer"
Through the Gap— "Poem Of Class"
Twigs— "Old Wolf"
Willow Springs— "In Killdeer's Field"

* *

"Communal," "Fete At Twilight," "Gaming," "Fishing For Home," "Flight," and "The Country In Which All Others Are But States Of Mind" collected in *demi-poems* (chapbook), Red Dancefloor Press, 1994.
"The Country In Which All Others Are But States Of Mind" and "Tornadium" reprinted in *Red Dancefloor*.
"Flight" reprinted in *Pegasus*.
"The Hunters" appeared in *Kentucky Poetry Review* in a different version entitled "The Human In The Earth."
"Man-Song" reprinted in *The Ledge*.
"Museum" reprinted and nominated for Pushcart Prize by *Unsoma*.
"Old Wolf" reprinted in *Best Poems of 1973, Borestone Mountain Poetry Awards 1974, A Compilation of Original Poetry Published in Magazines of the English-Speaking World in 1973*, Pacific Books, Palo Alto, CA, 1974.
"Sacred Cows" reprinted in *Back Home in Kentucky* and in the *Anthology of Magazine Verse & Yearbook of American Poetry 1986-1988 Edition*, Monitor Book Company, Beverly Hills, CA, 1988.
"What We Have Heard On High" reprinted in *Through the Gap, an anthology of contemporary Kentucky poetry*, 1990.

* *

Front cover photo by Cheri Kirkwood, "Killdeer's Field"
Back cover photo by Yee Ling Mui, "Three Statues"

for Forrest Ray Cope

1922-1943

~

because I was not there

to tell him

Sometimes . . . we thought too long a distance in advance
of our sounds, managed to achieve abstractions
(dim ones I grant), which we failed utterly to make known
to other folk. After all, language did not grow fast in that day.

—from *Before Adam,* Jack London

Contents

I

Man-Song	3
Aesop Come To Perch	4
Appalache	5
The Country In Which All Others Are But States Of Mind	7
Communal	8
Museum	9
What We Have Heard On High	13
Indian Summer	15
Flight	16
Sounding The Crane	17
A Burial	18
Gaming	19
Ohshon	20

II

The Hunters	23
Tornadium	31
The Ritual	33
Sleeping Out	37
Nightwalker	40
The Art Of Seeing	42
Old Crow	45
The Birds In My Window	47
Death Of W.	49
The Meaning Of The Moon	51
Old Wolf	52
Sacred Cows	54
Hunting With Professors	55
In Killdeer's Field	56

III

Fete At Twilight	61
Bar Verse	62
Taking My Country With Me	63
Freud	65
Tyros	67
The Fall Of '86	68
Poem Of Class	71
Looking For Boston	74
Fishing For Home	76
The Dig	77
Bells On The Mountain	78
Landover Beach	79
Pastoral	80
The Other Word	82
Once In A Blue Moon	84
Of Whitman, Reclining	86

IV

Playing The Thing Again	91

I

MAN-SONG

(played on sticks)

When your feet hit the ground, the others
will have gone, out of fear, running,

bare knuckles stone-smoothed by so many quick
retreats. But you will not run. You will

walk to the highground overlooking the fields.
You will look down on the others,

all humped like shallow pygmies in deep
hiding. But you will not hide. You will

roar out a word that means more than they know.
And they shall look up and marvel.

AESOP COME TO PERCH

In the trees we have
a saying: the surest
way to be killed is
to finish your banana.

There comes a feeling,
distant, all in all
a better language,
that could well be

the slow one,
the greedy one,
singing from the
grave, warning

of your coming.
We wait for
you for days
and would not be

the hairless hunter
even if
we could,
not give up

that fear, that
song that eludes you,
that betrays you
beyond your ken.

APPALACHE

Now I am on this high hill
to be to all creatures in the gutted wet valleys,
the tree-lined middle lowlands, visible, known.
I move and the eyes of an entire forest lift.
They focus and converge.
My image at once is in ten thousand places.
I go out through the land
in the seized brain of animals,
my smile in their foreheads.
They carry me, carry me, implanted, ingrained,
to their ground-nests and burrows.
They transport me lightly
to their dark dens and caves.
They impart my visage to the seeded trembling eye,
to the still-mind of the unborn
who dream of me, dream of me.
When they see me they shall know me:
I am on this high hill.

Even in the cities the thing I now am
will come to them like a thought,
like a dim recollection,
preceding me through the streets
until I'm known like the mountain I stand on,
until those who name me first,
whoever they are, wherever they are,
will rise like a wind in the earth's estimation,
until my birth is a symbol, my death a sign.

Even when all I do—though I can but think of this in bone—
is begin slowly to breathe,
not as I *have* done
but as the earth has done,
and every thought becomes one thought
and that the thought of the earth—
the same thought, the *only* thought,
the thought the wild dog has
when his belly's full of blood
and the air is cool
and it is dusk
and he leans upon his paws
wanting nothing—not even the truth.

THE COUNTRY IN WHICH ALL OTHERS ARE BUT STATES OF MIND

The hills are dark.
What's behind the hills is dark.
Something grows where the man
cannot go to or find.
It's deeper than any soil,
harder than any stone.
No one comes to this place in frills.

COMMUNAL

We found a cave and set up camp
in the burn of a slow fire,
our eyes uncannily red.
We crouched against the dark
and imagined other eyes
that could watch our every move.
None of us could speak.
None of us could sleep
or dream or think anything
one would be caught dead thinking.
And then the youngest sat up screaming
that he had been here before,
in a world back before his eyes,
that he had drawn with slate
upon these flickering walls
the victory of the hunt,
the glory of the kill,
the cold dark beyond the killing dark.
I leaned hard against
the cold, wet lip of the hill,
not knowing who he was
and, at the time, not caring—
until he learned to keep silent
in the face of these things.

MUSEUM

Whose voice was first sounded on this land?—
        Mahpiua-luta of the Oglala Sioux

Pond said three words
and she called it a song.
I broke a rock upon a rock.
Two ridges above the falls
I think there was a dog.

    ∧

I loved her dress.
It was long.
I loved beneath it
the cool and warm together,
the way all things became one thing
as I entered the

mound, pregnant

in the moon in a field
the city fathers
maintain for an indifferent public.

∧ ∧

Relics . . .

      the relics.

I fondle the beads,
soothe my hand
through the feathers,
and kneel at the
plate-glass-protected encasement
of arrow and spear heads,
tomahawks and knives.

Relics, it is said . . .
and in this uncertain light
there is no better name—

for my life,
my wife's,
my child's.

    ∧ ∧ ∧

*We talked for more and more hours
of nothing in particular—
like dying people anywhere.
When our night began to fall
we went out to the tall trees
to relieve ourselves.
There, sparrows jibed nervously.
Crows set up a chorus,*

*jeering at the hawks
that had begun to circle the sky.
Crickets and cicadas
ranted with tree-frogs,
and the wind whispered in the outermost leaves.
It was that restlessness in the air
that betrayed the coming darkness.
Long before we were conquered
we learned to climb a tree-vision,
run wild on a blade of grass.*

∧ ∧ ∧ ∧

But who can know this, after all?
Not the money-changers at the gate.
Not the tourist at the rail.
Not that one who checks the locks
and points us to the door.

Who is that one on his face
at the changing of the guard?
From where comes such singing?

That baby asleep—
is he milk of his mother?
Is he honey of his father?

Is he this? A part of

                    this?

∧ ∧ ∧ ∧ ∧

You do more than you know,
you too clad financiers
of such sacrosanct diversions.
You open a good wound
for those few like myself
who may come here, still breathing,
out of your most savage dreams,
out of some stone-aged forest,
desperately, desperately, remembering . . .

and saying
         under our dust:

Conjure this, night watchman,
and look well into the night.
We may one day soon howl
at that white lamb moon
lying gently above these iron gates,
may one day soon dance—
without paint, out feather,
out naked red skin,
past the moon to that good father of lights
who, alone, awaits our desperation.
We are here in this primitive
waiting for the change.
We are holding this earth together.

WHAT WE HAVE HEARD ON HIGH

In time, just
when you think you
have gone deep
enough into the forest,
someone will call your

name. You will turn,
amazed that you
are known even there,
will go on and go
out, saying:

I have heard nothing.
You are trained for that
after all, trained well to ignore
what you cannot
reasonably account for.

And there's no reason
in this, nowhere
to begin, nothing
to record or to regard
at your leisure:

you were alone and were
spoken to and the earth could not
have been more near
and you froze and for
an instant were as primitive

as stone. So you go
and will not return, ever,
in a million years.
You go back to the shops
and the tucked-away houses,

by and through strange apartments,
in and off diversions.
You go and are startled
by every slinking child
all-seeing from any window,

every stray cat and dog
appearing at your door,
the vagabond Indian,
the solitary crow.
You go and even sleep

cannot be what it was:
the eye closes,
the earth is young,
and you are huddled by a fire,
suspicious of every sound.

INDIAN SUMMER

My hand sings.
It is a bird.
I am a flock.
I am a chorus.

FLIGHT

The daybirds
huddle together.
The night crowds
them in. Then
with air to outlast
it in the hollow
of their bones,
they fly into
themselves,
into their own
dreamed-of sun
where the night
cannot reach them.

SOUNDING THE CRANE

Across the breaks
flew the crane I
could just hear the wings.

I was about to push off
but was
oh so in awe

so when the crane
had passed me by
I stayed on that silence—

beyond that was nothing.
I was still
in the wake

of what I had not heard
that irrevocable quiet
that nothing

when on the lake
just below me
some silly sons of bitches

broke with their squalls into
fire into
idiots with their guns.

And then how such silence—
falling with it,
falling with it.

A BURIAL

The dark within it hardening,
I shoulder the box
and speak to it.
I walk my limping shovel
back through the parted trees
and lean on it, null-minded,
beneath a struck pine.
A hawk's eye descends.
Who is that waiting on the road?

The dark within it deepening,
I heave it to heaven.
The sun is not changed.
No flutter of silver wings
to bear the box aloft.
No thunder of clouds.
I post it on the rocks
while I carve out a home,
the dark within it darkening.

GAMING

I still go sometimes
to lie drunk upon the rocks.
The cliffs reel above me.
The buzzards go round.

When they are close enough to smell,
I spit straight in their faces.
Go to hell, I say.
And off they do go.

OHSHON

Now I am brought to this edge
and have felt the unknown hand
grip the underside of my belly.
I have risen impaled,
unearthly posed,
thrust toward a kingdom.

I have tipped grasshopper wings
cross-ways in the sun
and have believed I was a bird.
I have stretched myself amazingly,
flown wide-turns of the soul.
But it is too much, too little . . .

Now I am brought to this edge
and have heard you howling from the water.
I have left the water running.
I have crawled to you on my knees.
I have licked your hand, waiting.
I am of whose kingdom, whose kingdom?

II

THE HUNTERS

(a poem for three voices)

3rd: *(Whistling, with a lump,*
       some mournful hillbilly tune,
       all else quiet as the dead)

1st: We sat in one corner of the evergreen earth

2nd: in back of the house.

1st: The corner next to the plum trees
       and the field of red clover

2nd: *this* side of the woods.

1st & 2nd: Daddy cleaned the squirrels.

2nd: Laughing brother and I

1st: laughed and I picked up the skins and
       cut off the tails and

2nd: teased the white cats.

1st & 2nd: Daddy whistled remembering:

(And while Daddy speaks, the 1st & 2nd voices
pick up the same mournful song)

3rd: I've always gone hunting, son,
fetching down squirrels
with my hand-me-down gun
and listening to them fall.
They reach for a savior
in the limbs of trees,
scaring the birds from
the cheap seats of the upper row.

1st: They reach for

2nd: a savior

3rd: in the limbs of trees,

1st: scaring the

2nd: birds from the

3rd: cheap seats of the upper row.

1st: But

2nd: Walt Disney's coming on!—

1st: so I would run, run,

2nd: run,

1st: cause I knew *he* loved animals.
I was the wild mountain trapper
with a pet black bear.
I did not kill him.
My heart was a mountain.

2nd: Your

3rd: heart was a

1st: mountain.

3rd: *(with a lump)* . . . I've always gone hunting, son . . .

      *

2nd: I said

1st: no, not that way.
   Not that way, Daddy.
   I have not yet told you.
   I cannot tell you, Daddy.
   Oh, Daddy, I will.

3rd: Oh,

1st: Daddy,

2nd: I will.

1st: I know where some are.
   And I know we could kill them.
   And I know if not kill them
   we could take them into our hands
   and they would know who we are.

3rd: They

2nd: would know who

1st: we are.

2nd: They would say,

1st: like this,

2nd: only not *just* like this,

1st: there is earth in your eyes,

2nd & 3rd: there is earth in your eyes,

1st: and in your hands also.

2nd: Your

3rd: heart is a

1st: mountain.

3rd: *(with a lump)* . . . I've always gone h—

                        *

1st: I was

2nd: up and still night
      and learning to walk easy
      and not to break branches
      cause they crack and scare squirrels.

1st & 3rd: They crack and scare squirrels.

1st: Learning to be quiet
 and to be quieter
 and to listen and . . . *to listen and . . .*

2nd: Mind how the fog just hangs there.

1st: It does.

2nd: And when we don't move,

1st: our breath just hangs there.

2nd: It does.

1st & 2nd: And we hang there, too,
 maybe hunting,

3rd: maybe nothing.

1st: I close my eyes tightly
 and am not me
 but Daddy hunting

2nd: (see him stepping where Daddy steps?)

3rd: but not quite

2nd: the same,

1st: never quite managing
 to breathe when he breathes
 or to not breathe

2nd: to *not* breathe

1st: when he says

27

3rd: Shhh!

1st: Trying so hard to *be* him.
       Sweat trickling down cause
       I am trying so hard and

2nd: Daddy listens so I listen, too.
       I close my eyes tightly
       and try to hear what Daddy hears.

1st: I try so hard.

3rd: I

2nd: try so

1st: hard.

2nd: I open my eyes
       and he's looking up

1st: so I look up and
       wonder what he sees.
       I look and look
       and am quiet and listen
       till sweat burns my eyes
       and I grit my teeth
       and hold on and hold on
       and I won't fail you, Daddy.
       Honest, I won't fail you.

All: Honest, I won't fail you.
       Honest, I won't fail you.

*

1st: It fell from the tree.
       A shower of chestnut leaves and fur
       floated down to the earth beside it.
       I shoved the low-lying branches away
       with the point of my gun and slid
       down the bank to claim it.

3rd: But it wasn't dead.

2nd: It wasn't dead.

1st: It was writhing, convulsing,
       the blood from its mouth
       painting red the leaves
       and the soft, pale-yellow baby down of its belly.
       So what was it made me stop
       to feel and taste
       that fall morning?
       or to know the steel of my gun
       so alive on my neck?
       or the thing at my feet
       gone so wildly from its body?

3rd: You came back. You saw.

2nd: One of its eyes was shot through
       and the other stared out at nothing
       and when you bent down to shut it

1st: a piercing *human* cry
       came up from below my hand.
       I stood quickly I was

29

2nd & 3rd: scared

1st: and dug my bootheel into its head.

3rd: Then what was it in the calm
or the commotion of that world
when the cry was soon forgotten?
when wrens bickered in the underbrush?
crows cawed, changing trees?
chipmunks resumed their tireless playing
in the leaves just away
from the way we would have gone,
from where nothing could have moved
though I commanded?

1st: I came back. I saw.
I will not need to look again.

TORNADIUM

It was that time of the
evening when
a neighborhood
least expects anything.
We were as tall as the sun.
Where the leaf
moved

was
fragile. Our fathers
in lawn chairs
lay back gently dozing
when the bottom
fell out
of the sky.

We saw its beginning,
how it turned
and breathed
and singled us out,
going mad
with the scent
of the weak

and the fearful
(or the strong and the brave)
who stood without question
forgetting their names,
grinning
like smacked
children.

I ran out
between houses
with more life
than I had known,
my feet doing a thing of
survival.
I was all I never

dreamed of.
I was more than I am.
I ran out between houses
with more joy than I had known.
I would have
gladly
shed my clothes.

Now the way to return there
(and I have known this always)
is to imagine
the one wind blowing,
the present wind,
as coming
from a far country

to remind me
of that nakedness.
I move,
I breathe,
I have my being
in a kind of
whirling, dipping past,

blown stark as the leaf,
swept outward,
upward,
dancing,
alive, turned
loose by a terrible
simplicity.

THE RITUAL

(Rev. 1:6)

1

Though we do not play well,
we play our best at those times
our lives most depend on it.
We play beyond ourselves.
We meet in a holy place,
my blond brother and I,
and sanctify ourselves
for that game which no other
in the living world can play:

we do a new thing
with checkers.

(Often, it happens.
Like priests we contain ourselves.
All words are unspoken
beyond the gunny sack veil.)

2

The past is a dampness.
The sun slowly cools.
My brother, the younger,
makes his first move.
Out of darkness I see him,

now, take on a light,
his skin incandescent.
Before my weakening eyes
he is growing a beard,
and I am not at all amazed.
He turns silvery-gray.
A body-sized heat
creeps over my shoulders.
I play in a fever
with moves not my own.

3

In a glow they are at home in
they come tapping canes.
They come meant for each other.
They come, not summoned,
but resident where we are.

They sit, are sitting,
with their Barlow knives honed
and their fresh blocks of cedarwood
waiting to be carved,
waiting, still, to be carved.

White pouches of tobacco
with yellow strings dangling
have not gone from vest pockets.
They are going to . . . are going to . . .
but have not rolled their own.

Mouth open, an old man
has half-told a story
that no one half-believes.
They have never yet believed it
in all these many years.

A child waits forever
to drop his horehound candy
through a crack in the spent floor.
I stare at him wildly,
my hair crawling backward.

And someone is quavering:
Five pounds of flour,
five pounds of meal,
shoestrings, peppermint,
a penny's worth, a penny's worth. . . .

4

My brother, think on these things:
oh the moves that we make
are so good, so good,
that no one must teach us;
we bring our lives to bear
every whit, every whit.
We do more than we can do,
are more than we can be,
vie, wholly living,
to resurrect the dead
and, my brother,
we are aged and capable.

5

King me, I hear my blond brother say.
King me, I say,
and we awake to ourselves:

a king is my brother,
I am a king,
we move backward and forward,
we jump the lean years.
On nights when a prayer
is not quite enough
it is substance we play for.
Lord, give us this day
more than dead images of our past—

let those images live.

SLEEPING OUT

We were to sleep, being children,
confined of green windows
that opened on the earth,
those in houses, once, above us.
They would flash at odd times,
go out, flash again,
while we in the tent
would feel a warmth that we knew
but could not know exactly.
(Someone looking to see
if, in fact, the nude earth
had not swallowed us whole
would stand in the breach
to eclipse the known world
and would spread a lesser light
upon us. We knew this as love.)

We waited, being children,
for that known love to blink out,
then came out of the tent.
My closed eyes were opened.
It was a kind of strange sleep
within which I managed
to exact just the right dream.
Secretly, silently,
feeling my eyes cross themselves
and go on, I came to the place
where the girls were.

*Take that breast in your hand,
man-child, man-child.
It is happening everywhere.
On mountains. In valleys.
On the banks of all rivers.
Being children, children
must blindly go blindly
into somebody's field,
must sleep first with the earth
and give to it. Sleep.*

The night air was changing.
The thought of it changed.
She came out of the center of darkness.
This close (and then closer)
I was struck by a fear
that, perhaps, in an instant
a sharp light would blink on,
that I would be caught single-handedly
doing a wrong thing
in the only wrong tent
in the neighborhood.
I had not known this trembling,
ever, in the day.

*Take that breast in your hand,
man-child, man-child.
It is happening everywhere.
Take it it in your hand.*

I turned from her,
praying that my friends
would walk past, knowing
they could never, now, save me.
I turned *to* her, fearing,
asking what love this was,
why no one had told me
or if, even, someone had.

Take that breast in your hand.

If it were true that this need
were mine only, mine only,
then should I not have been afraid?
What awakened inside me?
When is a child not a child?

Take that breast in your hand.

So I did, strangely.
Oh, I did.
I did.
And did.

NIGHTWALKER

I kept telling
the people
the night is
a slow train
of windows
that no one
looks out of.
I thought then
how wild that
must sound,
how strange
the night is
to insiders.

I went out
for my walk
as usual,
stepped up
on the fog bank
and into the eyes
that watched me.
Even Mrs. Bedlow,
with silver binoculars,
watched to see
what I would do.

It was all
in one movement.
Where the gentle

leaf stood
with its tree
turned up
against the chill,
I passed out
of their country.
I could hear
windows closing
everywhere.
I passed
through sleep
like a dream.
Mrs. Bedlow,
I wish you
could imagine.

THE ART OF SEEING

1

It was hard to convince the child
that the ocean was still there.
I took her down to where the wet would be,
scooped it up in my hands.
I splashed her hollow eyes.

Water pooled beneath her forehead.
She caught sunlight on a wave.
Laughed and turned a cartwheel
just missing old Logan, blind hermit
of these islands who just might be a child,

who waits for the sound of her to take shape
and do anything, shine, anything.

2

Logan: I once knew a man

who could see so precisely
nothing escaped him.
But everything kept changing.
He could never for the life of me
tell me what was there,
what was eternally there.
He would say:

*they used to be,
they used to be there. God knows
they were there the last time I looked.
They were standing on single legs
(with one wing over their eyes),
and when I spoke, God, they listened,
when I listened, God, they spoke.*

I can't say what he saw,
what he wanted me to see.
There was no life in his words—
men were sticks,
women sexless as stones.
I could not live in such a world.

3

And so I go on.
I spend my nights with the child
in and out of dreams and visions,
painting as best I can
what I hope she will see—
Dylan's heron priested shore,
Robinson's tooth sheathed in cloud,
the wind, the silent sails.
A child out to see the world,
out to come upon the world
in a simply reasonable way,
should be still and know
that the thing which she sees
is exactly the right thing,
the real, the necessary, thing.

4

And so I go on.
It's hard to think how it might have been
without days in the darkroom,
palming my eyes against the sun,

developing, regressing,
cursing my negatives for that one lost, empty sea,
the one with no waves falling upon the rocks like thunder.
It's hard to think how my world would have appeared.

OLD CROW

A pair of brown
Buster Browns

on a road, a gravel one,
from an old black-

patched Ford
to an early morning

auction spring
of dusty '54—

Grand-father,
I still love

you the smell
of your tobacco

the way you
looked in that

crowd of peasants.
Wait for me

in the crows.
What looked out

of them still
looks out of me.

What made them
black instead of red

makes my black heart
still adore you.

THE BIRDS IN MY WINDOW

I have decided to come live with you,
to go from my sick tree
where the mite-colored crows

have fled the real world.
They have declined since you saw them
and are failing more and more.

No longer do they curse
at the presence of strangers
or preen their dark absent feathers.

They look out at nothing,
no longer wary of the auger-eyed hawk
bristling on the wire.

The cat could leap at its pleasure;
the corn prospers in the field.
Was it you who suggested

I should clip the curled talons
that have grown into the limb?
No, not for a brace of quail,

not for a healthy tree.
I'll not be the one
who discovers them sleeping,

who moves them from their perch,
who lowers them to the ground.
Their own secret should contain them,

conceal them from the world,
until unnoticed, unremarked,
they go as gently as leaves.

DEATH OF W.

(on the tenth anniversary)

Now that W. seems finally
to have wasted away,
I must tell you why his room
would not want to give him up,
or why his window was broken
to get him out—
all three hundred pounds,
or four hundred pounds,
or however far it had taken him.
It had taken him,
thirteen years ago spring,
through bottles and cartons
and packages and cans,
and hours at the store
with only children to talk to.
I could not possibly
have known then
how much he loved our laughing,
or why he befriended children,
or why he taught us
of wild women
and backseat lovemaking.
But I could wish for him now
those same wild stories
told us in the backroom
racking bottles,
in the walk-in
pushing up milk,

bending low to steal a glance
at the milk-white thighs
of beautiful women—
all beautiful to W.
and all unattainable,
until alone in a room
that gradually grew smaller,
on a bed that grew accustomed
to the increasing depression,
that would have refused
the weight of some
slighter, softer form,
but received him easily,
lightly extending,
lifting its edges like arms
until it held him,
loving him.

THE MEANING OF THE MOON

Now we are here
and look off into the cars
and drive up and back down for days and days
and do not lift our eyes.

But now it is night.
We get out and go up and the moon is rising
in the alley. It is off to the left
and I think of a street lamp

somewhat yellow in fog.
I smoke.
The smoke rises and the moon does.
Now it is off to the right

and they are wanting me to go,
thinking, I suppose, that I am crazy.
But I am watching the moon rise
like a hot-air balloon.

I am thinking how its color
is like the belly of a frog:
you cut it open just right,
you lay open the vitals perfectly.

OLD WOLF

Although wolves don't often
come to howl outside my window,
last night one did. Just one,
while the others sat back
on haunches and watched his
moves, his circlings, his years
of experience. A circle,
trampled to the earth by
his restless feet, seemed
a deep well from my upstairs
window; and he, unable to climb
the snowy, wet walls of his prison
and, being old, too conditioned
to admit defeat, paced and sat,
always within the circle,
and raised his nose in the exact
same spot, and howled
at the same moon above
his head and mine—
until I slipped quietly down
the stairs to peep around
the curtain, in full view
of the truth. Then he was a wolf.
Old wolves have faces marred
by unrest and bad consciences.
But, after all, it's their life
to kill—and mine to stay alive.
So I shot him, in full view
of his starving family. And

they watched him growl and not
back down, and felt him knowing
that an old wolf must provide
for his own, one way or another,
himself or the man. But
I made him look like a failure.

SACRED COWS

I go out to try the cattle.
I could blow out the sun
of their liveliest calf

and their eyes would not change.
A god could leap
shorn of its blasted brain

and they would sit there still yawning,
chewing the air,
eyes blank as the sky

when a man's head explodes,
or does not explode,
or the world does or does not really end.

HUNTING WITH PROFESSORS

Dogs can do no better
on this night, toothed,
cold as an otter,

than to gather bones together,
or to congregate like wolves
and, howling, nose up

at the surrounding moon.
You curse them, you find yourself
barking like bitches

but without a place of love,
not here, not there,
no place in all the earth.

Talk, here, does not hold them.
They have come with their masters
but have forgotten who we are:

we are so far removed
nothing's left us
but to lean on our cars,

to pretend in the moonlight
that we know what's going on,
something we can almost remember.

IN KILLDEER'S FIELD

What we didn't
eat of it
took just hours to return,

propped at the end of
the long row
like some lurid

scarecrow
or like some three-legged
sawhorse with

a head toppling
on it.
I said Clover those damned eyes

and kept dropping in seeds.
Clover, too,
who'd shot it first,

only nodded that he'd seen, then
bent back to the hoe,
took more time

now with each hill.
Twenty feet
from where we'd skinned it,

leaving all but the hindquarter
to bloat in the sun
like some roadkill,

indecent, Clover
broke and ran.
But I stayed

to see it die again,
licking its gone leg,
the absurd white

of its nakedness
giving way
at the bone.

III

FETE AT TWILIGHT

Now the distant sun
hard by the moon
would not hang there
but for a certain

mesh of darkness.
We tip our glasses round
and toast our summer's
welded brew.

There is light in it.
There is dark in it.
Four drunk and westbound crows
are also in it.

BAR VERSE

(waiting on a bus)

As it turns out, the
wait has not been so bad,
has driven me to the books,
has bred in me a kind
of tolerance. When
I hear of poor Clover,
for example, lately
gone to drink, or Reverend
Swaggart's temptation,
I do not lift my head.
But when the church
boys come and go
and go roundabout our
table and hand us
tracts and verses
and ask if we know Jesus,
I say without thinking,
yes, I think we do.
When I ask if they know
Nietzsche they say
Nietzsche can't save
you and they are right
and I know it and I tell
them they are wise.

TAKING MY COUNTRY WITH ME

Delsey still
imagines that all
men are equal,
that nothing
is better than
equality on
a bus, going
south with
the pallid old
white men.
I watch them
reflected as
she courts them,
preening her
colors. I am
with her as
far as Tulane.

I was thinking
tonight that of all
the old south
that went by me,
I could tell
you nothing.
Just the earth
growing more
and more distant.
Just the world
I am out of,

retreating from
the need of anyone,
sustained by
a fixed isolation.
At 9:35 I deboarded
and have not
left my rooms.

FREUD

I was a white man in Birmingham
when the dog-dream awoke me.
It was more real than it could be.
I am less sure, in *my* dreams,
of the color of my skin
than I was in the dream of those dogs.

Free to do as I chose,
I climbed a tall hill.
Every light came out of hiding.
Every clearing was a sun.
Every tree fell away to make true
the dream of those dogs.

I pulled with both ears.
In the weeds right in front of me,
where even I could not believe,
something deep in its own darkness
was running. I came out of my ears
and into the dream of those dogs.

All I knew would not help me.
All I had seen would not.
I could not have imagined
in thirty-seven years
that this creature, not created, was here.
It was a dream of those dogs.

It came out and stood before me
in the perfect image of itself,

like a shadow in need
of attachment. I moved; it moved.
I turned; it turned
on the red eyes of those dogs.

Having no time to measure
my skin against the sun,
I fell, face down,
in one instinctive gesture
that any life could have depended on.
Breaking free of those dogs,

something dark slipped beneath me,
something alien came attached.
The dogs, in a day-lit frenzy
of howls, woke and vanished.
I lay trembling until nightfall.
I arose a universal man.

TYROS

I woke early this morning and tried to remember
how it was to believe in leisure. But that was hours ago.
Now I walk in the legacy of my stillborn will to power,
in a kind of historic trance, down Constitution Drive
and across to Mt. Vernon, measuring my steps
to exhaust the day, imagining the next war.
I return with the screams of children coming
out through the walls, wondering how they will cope
with this freedom, what illusion will ultimately cheat them.
It's like hearing young Sisyphus struggling in his sleep.

THE FALL OF '86

*Our present society, it seems to me, fosters two
undesirables: the gullible and the cynic.*
                —from an anonymous conversation

On the eighth leaning floor of Patterson Office Tower
a number of things are possible, but one is not at all likely.
I go there to stand alone where the vending machines are.
I look out the walled window.
                    Sometimes
there are birds, all sorts of flying birds, birds from relatively near,
relative birds from far, but most of the time, flying,
not a single resplendent bird in the whole flying scheme of things,
only students who, milling, going on and on below me,
lean against the wind and hold, in common,
to their matched hats and skirts. I watch them, without birds,
and wait for any one of them
to look, to just look, up at me.
                    Invariably
I am brought down: someone enters the room.
I hear the jingling of his change or the opening of her purse.
They drop their coins into the slot, pull the designated arm.
Something falls. They bend. They bend to pick it up
and I turn to see *her* bend—
the one unflying constant that draws me out and away.
I turn my back to the world.
                    Sometimes
they sit, when it is warm and not raining, around the fountain
in the square. Birds are there at such times, not near, but far,
high in the high locust that rises above and beyond.

If you could hear them, they would sing. If you could hear them,
they would laugh. At their books they would laugh,
like birds which beyond and above them sing.
Sometimes they speak—
                    "Do you really read Camus?"
                              I do not know the voice,
so of course do not answer. He could not be so alone.
The window is, I am, it is somehow a downed world
with superfluous wings,
          unable to even hover.
                         "Do you really read Camus?"
                                   He points a brown,
foreign finger at my stack of good books
and has not seen the birds. "I *have* read him," I could have said.
I wait for him to find his change, to drop his coins into the slot.
I wait to answer him only if I must.
                         "You–do–not–speak–in–galish?"
He speaks slowly, oddly, for the sake of my tongue,
and for an instant the bird breathes and is near unto laughter.
"Some," I say. "A little."
          "Then what of Camus?"
                                   "Yes, well,
he's dead now, after all, stone dead, seriously dead, has not spoken
a word in over sixteen years, has not risen from the dead.
What *could* I think of Camus?"
                    I might have seen
the bird turning, slowly, at a pace,
at the vast nearness of the sky.
               "The only truly great writer
of the century," he says. "The only truly believed."
                              I hadn't thought of it
that way, not precisely that way,
and it draws me out of the window from which the students have flown,

69

out of which the birds are reflected,
at night, and always, and forever, and today,
out of the room, to the elevator, from the elevator
to the ground. I leave him as simply
as I could take or leave Camus,
as Camus could have taken or left me.
                                    I go out. I am here. I am stopping
at the fountain. I am looking up at the window.
From such a distance, I'm afraid, it's so difficult to see,
so impossible to tell precisely what's going on.
I think I see a man, a dark-skinned man, a man, I suppose,
not meant to have a name, a man who appears to be—
I'm almost sure that he is—waving and grinning down at me,
a man who, headlong, at once bursts from the window, explodes
into light, and for an instant, even flies,
                                    and students, those students,
who don't know, I'm afraid, not now, not after this,
which way to turn, turning every which way,
some running for the phones, some screaming, some applauding,
                                                      and me,
still in my place, unmoved, unaffected, trying simply to decide
how the thing was performed, whether all things are possible
if one truly believes and is willing to be fanatic.

POEM OF CLASS

A look may
sometimes
turn
the
world
around,
like at noon
in the
hot-bed
of my
trade.
We loaded,
unloaded,
the antique
divanette
for the young
goddess
on the
balcony.
I strained
with all my
schoolboy
juts and
squares
to keep
its rare
skin
intact,
becoming,

at her
watch,
the most
gifted
and proclaimed
proletarian
of our
times.
I took on
with joy
the envy
of my
fellows,
I was
the best
by any
measure,
and up wound
flights
of stairs
I bore
the brunt
of her
inspection
without
a groan.
In the
tired cab
going home
I kept
to that
vision,

both hers
and
mine,
and have
come,
unwillingly,
to the
burden
of all
my days:
what I want,
what I
need
in this
life,
is someone
always
well above
me, deigning
to look
down,
if only
just to
see me
throw
back my
head.

LOOKING FOR BOSTON

Met her parents on Beacon Street,
my young shoulders bare,
Camel-rolled tee-shirt
from some 50's Neanderthal,
duck-tailed and out of time—
yes, I would move their piano.
Over it all she was singing
when on the stairs they spoke of need
as though the chuckle-headed servant
had bought the wrong tickets,
brought round the wrong car.
Always the wrong place, you see—
isn't that just the way?
Hill people were so unrefined
and *just too too too too.*

I left well into the dark,
out beyond the bridge
onto the path agreed upon
by more adept men at large.
How did I know they were defeated men?
those dozens out before me,
even one Maharishi gone off into the moon
to spend the night
lotus-eared and humming?
So content they seemed then,
so at home where they were.

At the water I must have cried
at that great hollow rustling
in the keep of the reeds,
the wind on the low boards,
the first chair viola who toiled in tears
at the sorrow and the mystery of her hands.
Dying of time and Tchaikovsky
I stood still in the pared doorway
amazed at the extent of song.
When she asked if I would help her—
the music over and me standing there—
I could think of no greater irony.
Such a puzzle, all those days,
such no way of knowing how *not* to appear
when I returned, no richer,
to the common Kentucky fields,
no poorer to the music of crows,
tossing hay above my head as if nothing
in the world had ever crossed my mind of going.

FISHING FOR HOME

I cannot know better than the moon on black water.
I can see no farther than the night heron
perched on that shadowy sleeve.
Still I swear my eyes are counted.
Something in the way I am to be here or nowhere,
in the way silence fills the boat and I have no desire.

THE DIG

We dug up his
god. Herr Wagner's
hand trembled as

he smoothed back
the gold of its
shoulders. This

man who for years
had been combing
the earth with his

madness. This
knee-crawler of
tombs and denizen

of ancient
ruins. Said:
this is what

the gods are
this is what
the gods are.

BELLS ON THE MOUNTAIN

You don't ever have to play for me.
When I hear you chiming through the walls
I'll put my ear up against
and hum along with.
That's really all I ask—
to be no farther than that,
no closer than the wings,
the quiet receding
just over the last hill,
the echoed soft ringing
faintly heard in the leaves,
dimly felt along the branches,
carried from the shore
to the outlying, trembling sea.
If I seem to be running,
I am not. To be *there*
would be the man
indifferent to the song,
tugging the trailing rope,
having spat into a corner,
wiped the eggs from his beard,
and merely glanced
at the white-collared nod in the doorway.
It is time, as usual,
but here at the edge
and the mystery of the world
it is always time, always.

LANDOVER BEACH

We are strangers off the water.
Morey, the lank fisherman,
peers out on the swelling sun
and dreams of spouting whales.
Marlowe, the sailor,
sees his own naked vision
bathing in the drench,
her dark nipples rising.
I'm a builder of ships.
The naive girls and boys
from the lop-eyed row of huts
dance circles at my feet
and sing out at the swan-sails
in the blue distance
of the splintered wharf.
They watch for me to come.
They fill up my going.
They know that in *my* dream
I've climbed with them the crag
to believe everything at once,
the present, the future,
together. In their eyes swim
the glories of all my first sea, —
nothing is so lovely. But
when I wave to them in leaving
I have not told them of the years,
nor how the sea becomes somehow
always less than it was.

PASTORAL

I was in a field in a summer
too long to tell.
I held something warm in my hands,
something that spoke another language

never told me.
I set it in weeds in a hollow place
where something had been.
I wanted it to move. It did not move.

I lifted it softly
and spoke something I cannot remember,
something about the sky.
That done, I had done everything

I knew how to do
and I stood there and waited.
Cow bells tolled in the valley
and the thing in my hands

became timeless, I swear.
Its last breath
became my breath
and I am still breathing and breathing,

am standing over this hollow
in my thirty-ninth year
waiting for the thing to move,
waiting to move with it,

for the moving thing to be gathered
from the tops of tall pines,
from nests, from burrows,
bone, tooth, and claw all coming undone,

skin coming undone,
every wild thing that had fed on it
giving it up,
coming apart in its time,

waiting for the man
to do a thing he has never done,
to find within his hands
much more than he expected:

life he can bleed back into it,
life he can give back to it.
That done, he
will have done everything.

THE OTHER WORD

There is a moment with the dying
when a living man must break for a window.
I did, and unveiled it.

A miracle of sun broke.
All eyes turned toward it.
The eyes of the dying, even, came alive

and turned toward it,
as if a savior had entered the room.
I looked for light in the faces

of men and women I had known
only vaguely all the days of my life.
I listened for a voice

that could shout down the walls
or give meaning to a silence.
I cleared my throat like a god.

Then I looked and that one
who had called me here looked.
He was dying, now, differently.

All the air in his body
rolled out of his mouth
like a word he could not have spoken,

like a wild, a savage, a primordial word
from the heart of a gentle beast
we had felled in Killdeer's Field,

going, going, pawing at the earth
for a foothold of light,
sun-reaching beyond belief,

choking on what,
in this life,
he most wanted to tell me.

ONCE IN A BLUE MOON

Some three A.M.'s are more
truthful than others;
that is, if you let them,
they grow more like eternity
than a thousand dark years.
You might hear horns
all around you suck back
into cars, disappear,
the blast inside-out;
or windows close or
doors lock themselves;
or every parking lot more
still than the field
it once swallowed.
Or all at once streets
may vanish and all "WALK"
signs, conspicuously,
fl-ash-ash as in mirrors.
If you are seated on
a roof ledge or a window
sill or scaffolding,
your cream ale beside you,
and you don't mind the cold,
once in a blue moon
even snow begins to fall.
You might just drift
with it, slowly turn
to white, your eyes

filling up with water
more ways than you know.
And not until the road
crew comes scraping
and tearing is there
anyone left in the world.

OF WHITMAN, RECLINING

O the bright morning
upon the dark, secret alleys!
O the empty flask!
O the cycled life
and the smell of good rot
in the pits of round cities,
the most fruitful of dead seeds.
It recalls me you, Walt Whitman,
O sleepy Walt Whitman,
that kind of perverse
and annoying beauty.
You fell to this earth
like an overripe peach—
full, having drunk so deeply.

I turn to you, ripening,
toast your gray beard,
and write this imperfectly, lazily.
It is enough, you would have said,
enough to still sing
with the same misapprehension,
the same wonder of an Adam
at the newness of his eyes.
What creation is this?
What a world is this?
If I am all that I feel,
I have lived through the ages,
am no less Whitman than McTeague,

contain the whole filthy,
cluttered, bloody world in a breath,
so cannot but look out at beauty.

It is enough, you would have said.
It has to be.

IV

PLAYING THE THING AGAIN

I

130 years late I show up to die in battle. I bring with me old maps of old Virginia and the best and worst wishes of every country on earth

and every state in this country and every county and every town. I bring with me all their good sons rolled up into one, some of whom

couldn't find Virginia, and all their good intentions, and all their good daughters held tight in my groin, and all their good rock-and-roll, free

verse, bad dope, hollow faces. I bring with me black and white slaves and black and white slaves to no one. I bring black and white pent-

up emotions, black and white guilt and greed. And the gratitude and the ire and the ignorance of John Doe. And the love of carpenters,

lumberjacks, carpetbaggers, drugstore owners, table bussers, grocery sackers, gas pumpers, book writers, and ten-million-and-one

dreamed-up software programs of ten-million-and-two stragglers eager to have a go. I bring with me a uniform no one of them has yet

seen, made of fabric not yet imagined, gaudy as a Zouave as with the dried blood of future martyrs. I bring a flag of fifty stars, and every

star a prophecy. I bring fifth-grade-primer words with intimations only a knower knows, with fire out of everywhere, with only god-

high birds, with the whole field from the hawk's vantage a cataract
billowing and stretched out for miles, wispy cotton tree-high.

Because this is how it happened, a stab at form, at order, but only a
stab, because *dis*-ordered is what war is. I see the top of my head

bob-bobbing above the ground-clouds, a red X upon it, amid a drove
of other X'ed-out heads lit up like a gameboard. I begin to see,

vaguely, the circumstance and the agent that will be the means to my
end: the onslaught and the general who knows well my kind, my

dog-eyed obedience, a whole troop of dog-eyes as willing as I to do
the unbelievable thing; that look in our eyes means we will try

anything many times until we know what else to do, means we have
come out of love and wonder to do the unlovely thing, the

hysterically mad thing, the unholy or holy thing we will tell no one of
but in dark words and phrases, means our lack of understanding will

drive us deaf dumb and blind, will empower us to rush headlong into
the mouth of a cannon, into powder-smoke and fire, into Hell or

Heaven at the barked words of a saint or an idiot.

II

. . . So I will be a slave.

III

When one begins, finally, to have no reason to sleep, the knelling of
the hour has no meaning. If it's morning—well and good. There'll

be people to see—doctors, bill collectors, civilians of that sort—
important things to say, news of the war to expound on and reiterate

and fume over. One might even suggest that at some future date will
occur some grand consolation, some reclaiming of my Fort Sumter,

some victory at Richmond, Vicksburg, some assassination or
surrender, some proclamation or some other dimly-hoped-for

expedient that will marshall us again. If it's afternoon—fine. One
can stand still in the muck and tip one's hat to strangers or take a day-

carriage downtown to be tempted by considerations one never has at
home. Like what possesses wry pigeons to conduct themselves as

they do, strutting and fussing and clucking so disdainfully as one is
conveyed beneath the sills? Or what imbues that stately courthouse

one always must pass no matter how one regrets it? Or where's the
source of one's anguish for those three old lonely men, all fashioned

in blue, on that precisely wrought and frescoed and white-washed
iron bench under that glorious courthouse elm, when all one really

wants to do is sit quietly there among them, to be simply affable and
bland, to note that the sun's really relatively warm but that one fears

the impending storm, and to remind them that very soon drab gray
winter, I swear, will strip them even of their minds? And then if it's

night—that's good as day. No civilian to visit, no day-carriage to rent, no thought quite so demeaning as those pointless day-thoughts

permitted one downtown. There's just this wisp of a gentle breeze feeding in at the window, and one does like to reflect upon the

stillness of the hour. Where else would one rather be than amid his own particular shadows, at his own particular end, breathing as

fearsomely and as lustfully as was ever his wont, but noting the fact with indifference,—since he happens now to expect nothing, and

looks for no better circumstance than what he has already seen, one's failing his own country, one's own God failing him?

IV

So I will be a . . .

V

I tell you what my duty is. I'll get me a Rodman or a Whitworth, maybe a 30-pounder Parrot, and shoot every mean bastard that aims such at me. How'd you

say to work this thing?

VI

I found a hand in a field. The hand had three fingers. Two fingers had no skin. I went around asking if anybody'd lost a hand. One said I lost my whole damn

brother.

VII

With more urges in one night than old gray-hairs in a year boy-soldiers lay on their sides, beat their manhood into the ground,

whittled away at their own substantial wars, arose weak-kneed and sleepy to be hurled into the earth at last, oh at last!—their virgin

bloods spilling out and running together, future families, cities, planted on red hills, would-be mothers empty shells. So know now

the grass.

VIII

And now the slave . . . the slave . . .

IX

July is such a troublesome month, people die in it. So when they ask me when would I like to die I say let it be now, and here (before the

right ragged poet comes, down-headed and amazed) in my own
house, my own bed, my own Old Dominion, and let me be alone

with my already broken body, blue hands folded nicely upon my
winter-white breasts, my blackberry quilt, since I am cold now always,

even in July, even as child-armies gather like flies around my right
and natural and silent decay—Northerns at my feet, Southerns at my

head—and smoke, dust, and fear ascend to my wide window, hang
there sweet as clover before my last few heaving breaths somehow

take it all in. And I *will* take it all in. I will go as they go, all these
children of my children, I will not live without them. I will comb

back my white hair that I might see more clearly how to join their
mad game, see all that consumption down Rt. 29, Red Roof Inns and

Days Inns and Ramada Inns and Wal-Marts and golden arches and
Shoney's just over the horizon, and Battleview Parkways hurling

traffic from D.C., see whiskered senators and congressmen lined up
on the rises with soft parasoled ladies, titillated by death. And no

doubt I'll let the sun in just one time too many to see how this
particular time goes. Beauregard or McDowell or Manassas himself

might just value such a view, might peer out over this land to survey
what comes of bondage. . . . Little soldiers, little hot and sticky

soldiers, blood or blackberry stains on all your mouths and hands,
bring your real guns and meet me here on my mountain, behave

nobly, shoot out your brother's eyes.

X

. . . . ?

XI

Atlanta burned. After that, in my legend, still there beside my father, my mother still next to him, I wondered how much of *our* lives had

gone up in flames, how often reenacted against the unchanging, unchangeable backdrop of our past. Our thoughts drifted off like

smoke into the dark above the stage. The night slowly dissolved us.

XII

. . . So I will be a slave, I said. I will finally be a slave. My ancestors will not have fought for the south. I will not house a bugle boy, a

color-bearer, a general, who speak when I speak, dream when I dream, lie still in the toil and quiet of my hands. I will not be justified

when the Stars and Bars is unfurled, when Old Glory is raised, when the pride in my father's eyes ennobles my heart. I will be a slave. I

will not know what it is at the name of Robert E. Lee that makes my heritage sufficient, that raises my dead. My father will be hanged, my

mother traded, my sister raped before supper. I will long but for a horse to take my love for a ride. I will not know where my grave is.

XIII

... So I will *not* be a slave. Maybe I will *not* be a slave.

XIV

You are white, I said, even if your brown Malawi skin *is* soft as summer. There is a difference here. You are white. An accident of

the sea. Or is this what God said? or my neighbor said? or *she* said? ... in her Liverpoolian brogue, with her tambalas and kwachas

spread out on the table, her travel-book of Blantyre, of the Great Rift Valley, of the Chewa, Nguru, Nyanja, and Yao. But what grew out of

our fumbling was an unbordered country. We breathed the same sky—or together dreamed the same blue encircling dome up and

over our heads. Our children were not black, not white, but sun-colored, well fed, laughing, simply good, the best of all civilizations

flowering inside them, lifting leaves and branches too great, too encompassing, to be plucked off, uprooted, burned down,

displaced,—all this a perfect garden we were planting with words as other lives not yet born called us out to bless the seeds, in all the wide

green mansion not a thought for the future, where they would wander to find love or withdraw to find peace, where they would hide to

escape the slave traders, what wars they would lose. We thought simply how each of them stood bathed in a light, forever like Correggio's

angels. Of the country of Earth. And no other, if not that.

XV

And no other, if not that—So no other? At last we are not soldiers. We stand like stage extras in a spinning field, leaning on ourselves,

trying to understand what it is we are now. In every direction is a place we can go, but like suddenly freed animals we still wear our

cages—some a deer's, some a killdeer's.

Printed in the United States
2788